MORETON-IN-MARSH TO WORCESTER

Vic Mitchell and Keith Smith

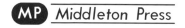
MP Middleton Press

*Cover picture: Recorded near Wyldes Lane, Worcester, on 25th July 1961 was no. 7007 **Great Western** departing with a Hereford to Paddington express. No. 4945 **Milligan Hall** (right) will follow it with freight from Stourbridge Junction to Stoke Gifford. (W.J.Probert/Millbrook House)*

Published January 2004

ISBN 1 904474 26 8

© Middleton Press, 2004

Design   David Pede
Typesetting   Barbara Mitchell

Published by
           Middleton Press
           Easebourne Lane
           Midhurst, West Sussex
           GU29 9AZ
Tel: 01730 813169
Fax: 01730 812601
Email: info@middletonpress.co.uk
www.middletonpress.co.uk

Printed & bound by MPG Books Ltd, Bodmin, Cornwall

CONTENTS

INDEX

ACKNOWLEDGEMENTS

We are grateful to many of those mentioned in the credits for their assistance and also to W.R.Burton, C.L.Caddy, D.Clayton, L.Crosier, G.Croughton, J.Day, S.P. Derek, G.Heathcliffe, J.B.Horne, M.A.N.Johnston, N.Langridge, C.Morgan, Mr D. & Dr S.Salter, G.T.V.Stacey, M.Turvey, and finally our ever helpful wives, Barbara Mitchell and Janet Smith.

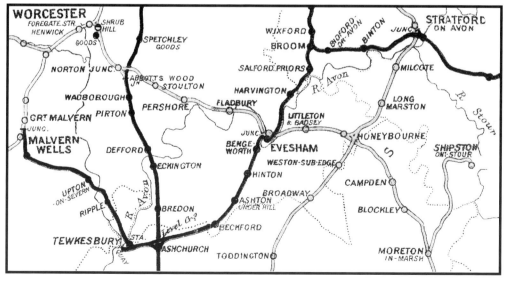

I.   Railway Clearing House map of 1947.

GEOGRAPHICAL SETTING

The route commences on Jurassic Lias and Oolitic Limestones which form the Cotswold Hills, passing through the Oolite in Campden Tunnel. Thereafter there is a long descent on Lias Clays across the Vale of Evesham, an area noted for its fruit and vegetable production.

From Evesham to Pershore, the line is in the vicinity of the River Avon and passes over several of its tributaries thereafter. It enters the Severn Valley on its approach to the ancient city and market centre of Worcester.

The maps are to the scale of 25ins to 1 mile, with north at the top, unless otherwise indicated.

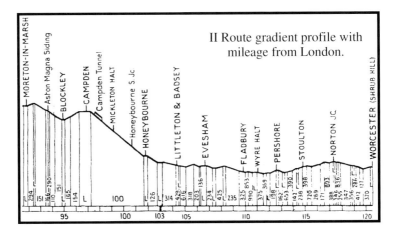

II Route gradient profile with mileage from London.

HISTORICAL BACKGROUND

The first railway to Worcester came from the south on 5th October 1850 in the form of a short branch from the Midland Railway's Birmingham to Gloucester line. It was worked by the MR, but belonged to the Oxford, Worcester & Wolverhampton Railway. The latter was granted its Act on 4th August 1845, the Worcester-Evesham section opening on 1st May 1852, with Evesham-Oxford following on 4th June 1853. The associated routes came into use thus: from Worcester north to Droitwich in 1852 and south to Malvern Link in 1859, from Evesham south to Ashchurch in 1864 and north to Redditch in 1868, and from Honeybourne north to Stratford-upon-Avon in 1859 and south to Cheltenham in 1908.

Most of the route featured in this album was opened as a single line, but was doubled during its first year. Each track was laid with three rails, but the broad gauge was never used regularly and was lifted after 1st April 1869. The OWWR had become part of the West Midland Railway in 1860 and this was absorbed into the Great Western Railway in 1863. This company was nationalised in 1948 to form the Western Region of British Railways.

Regular passenger services were withdrawn from the adjacent lines thus: north and south of Evesham in 1963, south of Honeybourne in 1960 and north thereof in 1969.

Singling of the route between Moreton-in-Marsh and Evesham took place on 20th September 1971 and on to Norton Junction on 25th October of that year, leaving a passing loop only at Evesham.

Privatisation resulted in Thames Trains Ltd. operating most services from 13th October 1996. The 7½ year franchise soon came under the control of the Go-Ahead Group plc., but it was announced in November 2003 that the franchise would be transferred to the First Group in April 2004. This already operated First Great Western services and it planned to create Greater Western to provide all trains from Paddington.

PASSENGER SERVICES

LONDON, OXFORD, KINGHAM, EVESHAM, and WORCESTER.—Great Western.

Down. — **Week Days.**

Miles from Oxford	Down.	mrn	mrn	mrn	mrn	mrn (Saturdays only.)	mrn	aft	mrn	mrn (Via Stratford-on-Avon.)	mrn
	98 London (Pad.) 126 dep.				5 30		9 45			11c10	1120
	98 Reading "				6 18		10 35				1 5
	98 Didcot "				6 52		10 15				1 7
—	Oxford dep.				7 35		11 14		11 35		1 57
3¾	Yarnton				7 44				Bb		2 6
7	Handborough, for Blenheim				7 52				11 51		2 13
13¼	Charlbury				8 4				12 2		2 23
17	Ascott-under-Wychwood				8 12				12 10		2 31
18¾	Shipton A				8 18				12 15		2 36
21¼	Kingham 130				8 30		11 46		12 25		2 41
25¾	130 Chipping Norton arr.				9b7		12a22		12b43		
45½	130 Cheltenham Spa B "				9 40				2 19		
24	Adlestrop				8 37				12 31		
28¼	Moreton-in-Marsh 78		7 30		8 49		11 59		12 42		
31½	Blockley		7 35		8 56				12 49		
33¾	Campden		7 42	m	9 3				12 56		
38¾	Honeybourne 126, 127		7 52	8 39	9p23		12 14	1230	1 6	2 1	
47¼	127 Stratford-on-Avon arr.		8 23		10 19		1 7		2 21	1 22	
	126 Stratford-on-Avon dep.				8 52		10 45	12 0		1 40	
40¾	Littleton and Badsey		8 0	8 45	9 27				1 13	2 7	
43¼	Evesham 623	7 5	8 8	8 50	9 36	1115	12 24	1239	1 22	2 12	
46¼	Fladbury	7 11	8 14		9 43			1245	1 30		
49	Pershore	7 16	8 22		9 51	1125		1251	1 38		
51¼	Stoulton		8 28		9 57			1256	1 44		
53¾	Norton Junc. 555, 560		8 34		10 4			1 1	1 51		
57	Worcester C' 116, 120 arr.		8 40		10 10	1137	12 43	1 7	1 55		
65¼	120 Malvern (Great) arr.		9 14		10b48		1 20	2b9	2 51		
86¼	120 Hereford "		9 48		12 0		2 17	3 0	3 45		
62½	116 Droitwich Spa "		9k5		10k55	1155	1 4	2B4	2 18		
72	116 Kidderminster "		9k24		11k11	1212	1 25	2B20	2 38		
90¾	116 Wolverhampton D "		11 2		12 51	1 0	3 0		3 50		

Down.	(Thursdays and Saturdays.)	aft (Worcester, Malvern, Hereford, Droitwich Spa, and Kidderminster Express. Luncheon Car for Passengers to Worcester and beyond.)	aft (Wednesdays and Saturdays.)	aft (Luncheon and Tea Car to Worcester.)	aft	aft (Via Stratford-on-Avon.)	aft	aft (Worcester, Malvern, Droitwich Spa, and Kidderminster Express.)
98 London (Pad.) 126 dep.		1245		1 45		2c10		4 45
98 Reading "				2 30				4A55
98 Didcot "					2 52			5 23
Oxford dep.				3 10	3 40			6 0
Yarnton					3 49			
Handborough, for Blenheim					3 56			
Charlbury					4 7			
Ascott-under-Wychwood					4 15			
Shipton A					4 21			
Kingham 130		2c17		3 38	4 32			
130 Chipping Norton arr.		2c43			5b18	4 51		
130 Cheltenham Spa B "		3c25			6 12			
Adlestrop					4 38			
Moreton-in-Marsh 78				3 51	4 50			6c34
Blockley					4 56			
Campden				4 1	5 3			
Honeybourne 126, 127					5 13	5 30	5 35	
127 Stratford-on-Avon arr.				4h56	6 2			
126 Stratford-on-Avon dep.							5 5	
Littleton and Badsey					5 23		5 41	
Evesham 623			2 50	4 16	5 35		5 45	
Fladbury			2 57		5 45			
Pershore			3 4	4 26	5 55			
Stoulton			3 10		6 1			
Norton Junc. 555, 560			3 15		6 7			
Worcester C' 116, 120 arr.		2 55	3 20	4 37	6 12			7 5
120 Malvern (Great) arr.		3 15	4 36	5 0				7 29
120 Hereford "		3 55	5 40	5 57				8 30
116 Droitwich Spa "		3 18		4 57	6 35			7 26
116 Kidderminster "		3 37		5 19	6 57			7 46
116 Wolverhampton D "		4 51		7 4	8 0			9 5

Down. — **Week Days**—*Continued.* — **Sundays.**

Down.	aft (Runs to Cheltenham Spa (arr. 8 6 aft.), see page 126.)	aft	aft	aft (Dining Car.)	aft (Via Stratford-on-Avon.)	aft	aft (Wednesdays and Saturdays.)	Sundays mrn	Sundays mrn (Luncheon and Tea Car, Paddington to Hereford.)	Sundays aft (Third class only.)	Sundays aft
98 London (Pad.) 126 dep.			4 45	6 5	6e10				1010		4 10
98 Reading "			4A55	6 50					11 0		5 2
98 Didcot "			5 23	6 52					1043		4 40
Oxford dep.			6 8	7 30					1155		5 52
Yarnton											
Handborough, for Blenheim			6 22	7 43					12 8		6 8
Charlbury			6 34	7 53					1218		6 20
Ascott-under-Wychwood			6 43								
Shipton A			6 49	8 3					1228		6 31
Kingham 130			7 0	8 12					1235		6 39
130 Chipping Norton arr.			7b23	8b35	8J25						
130 Cheltenham Spa B "			8q58	9 55							8q32
Adlestrop			7 6						1242		6 45
Moreton-in-Marsh 78	6 45		7 18	8 24					1253		6 56
Blockley	6 52		7 25	8 30					1 0		7 3
Campden	6 58		7 32	8 35				m	1 7		7 9
Honeybourne 126, 127	7 5	7 12	7 45		9 8			8 52	1 20		7 20
127 Stratford-on-Avon arr.			8b15								
126 Stratford-on-Avon dep.		6 47	7b15		8 45						
Littleton and Badsey		7 18	7 51			m					
Evesham 623		7 26	8 0	8 49	9 20	9 45	1010	9 5	1 29	6 50	7 31
Fladbury		7 33	8 8			9 52	Aa	9 12	1 36	6 58	7 38
Pershore		7 40	8 16	8 59		9 58	1024	9 23	1 43	7 7	7 46
Stoulton 560											
Norton Junction 556,											
Worcester C' 116, 120, arr.		7 51	8 27	9 12		10 9	1035	9 40	1 54	7 19	8 0
120 Malvern (Great) arr.				9 32				11 4	2 22		8 26
120 Hereford "				1021				1 40	3 5		
116 Droitwich Spa "		8 14		9 33				11 5	2 52	7 37	8 33
116 Kidderminster "		8 43		9 56				1133	3 12	7 51	8 56
116 Wolverhampton D "		1011						1237	4 13	9 20	9 59

NOTES.

- A Station for Burford (5 miles).
- A Reading (West).
- Aa Stops at 10 17 aft. on Saturdays to set down on notice being given to the Guard at Evesham.
- B St. James
- B Thursdays and Saturdays, via Worcester (Foregate Street).
- Bb Stops at 11 43 mrn. to take up on giving notice at the Station before 11 5 mrn.
- b Motor Car, one class only.
- C' Shrub Hill.
- c By Slip Carriage.
- D Low Level.
- d Except Thursdays.
- h Via Evesham.
- k Via Worcester (Foregate St.)
- m Motor Car, one class only.
- p Arrives Honeybourne at 9 10 mrn.
- q Via Honeybourne, one class only.
- U Slip carriage, via Banbury. One class only.

1. Timetable for September 1925

Down trains running on at least five days each week are considered in this section.

The 1850 timetable showed Worcester receiving six weekday and three Sunday trains on the MR branch from Wadborough. This section will not be considered further in this volume.

The first OWWR trains from Oxford comprised only a few coaches of its own, most of the trains being formed of LNWR stock running from Euston via Bletchley. The two sections were joined at Handborough. This arrangement lasted until September 1861.

The table below indicates the number of down trains in selected years.

	Weekdays	Sundays	
1853	5	2	
1869	5	2	(a)
1889	6	2	(a)
1909	8	3	(a)
1933	12	2	(b)
1949	10	4	(c)
1969	7	3	(c)
1989	11	6	(d)
2003	15	12	(e)

(a) Two extra weekday trains from Stratford-upon-Avon on weekdays joined the route at Honeybourne.

(b) Three of the weekday trains started at Moreton-in-Marsh.

(c) Five more trains between Honeybourne and Evesham from Stratford-upon-Avon.

(d) Included a Brighton to Edinburgh train on Sundays.

(e) One peak time London service was provided by First Great Western.

1. Fire Services College
MORETON-IN-MARSH

2.   The Moreton-in-Marsh World War II RAF training airfield evolved into a Home Office fire-fighting training centre in the 1950s and became a college in July 1981. Among many environments created was one featuring railways. No. 73126 is in this view, the first of three from 14th August 2003. (M.J.Stretton)

3.   The proportion of stock owned by the college diminished from 2000 onwards as Cotswold Rail Ltd stored an increasing number of coaches and locomotives on the site. A platform and level crossing were provided for training exercises and many lengths of track were laid on the old runways. (M.J.Stretton)

4.   Cotswold Rail act as retailers for redundant stock and large numbers of class 141 "Pacers" and sleeping cars have come and gone from the site. The firm also hires out locomotives, notably class 08 and class 47 diesels to Anglia Railways. All are moved by road. (M.J.Stretton)

5.   W.S.Gilbert would have appreciated the irony of a locomotive *travelling by road* from the Cotswolds to work in the Eastern Counties. Numbered 200, *The Fosse Way* was photographed at Ipswich on 6th December 2002. The livery is grey, with a logo in blue and red. (R.Adderson)

2. Moreton-in-Marsh to Worcester Shrub Hill

MORETON-IN-MARSH

III.   The main line from Oxford is at the bottom and the single line curving at the top is the southernmost part of the Stratford & Moreton Tramway. This was horse worked from 1826 until 1889 by which time it had become part of the GWR. A conventional passenger service was then operated to Shipston-on-Stour. This ran until 1929, but freight continued until 1960. The branch is extensively illustrated in *Oxford to Moreton-in-Marsh*. The map is from 1885 and shows the proximity of the station to the High Street.

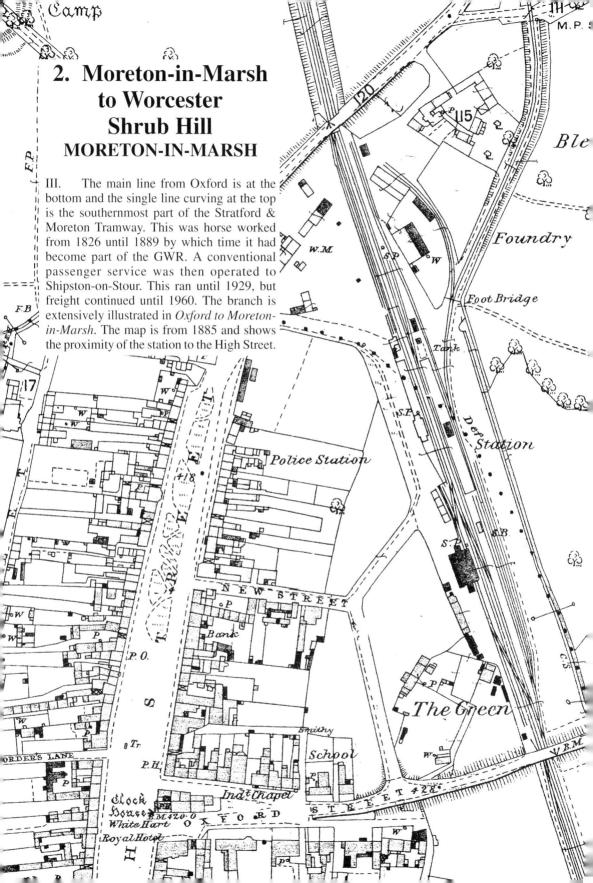

6.   The station was extensively rebuilt in 1872-73 to the form seen in this northward view. The original buildings had been cheap timber affairs. Cast iron was used for the urinal on the right. (Lens of Sutton)

7.   Contrasting brick courses and stylish chimney stacks gave a pleasing ambience, which was negated by the horse droppings at the entrance. The horse is facing the gates to the cattle dock. (Lens of Sutton)

8.   The bridge had to be provided with four flights of steps, as it also carried a public footpath. In the left background is the former headquarters of the Stratford & Moreton Tramway. (Lens of Sutton)

————————▶

9.   Pausing with a Worcester to Paddington express on 7th August 1923 is 4-4-2 no. 102 *La France*. This was one of three De Glehn compound 4-4-2s built in France and used for trial purposes. This example ran from 1903 until 1926. (H.G.W.Household/NRM)

————————▶

10.   Stock for local services stands in the yard, while a group of passengers waits for a down train. The number of residents grew from 1374 in 1901 to 1935 in 1961, while the number of passengers diminished. (Lens of Sutton coll.)

──────────▶

11.   In this northward view from the footbridge, vans stand at the dairy's dock on the right, while others wait at the goods dock on the left. There is a pit near the water column for the benefit of drivers of inside cylindered locos. (Lens of Sutton coll.)

12.   An unusual train arrived on the afternoon of Saturday 31st August 1952, hauled by ex-MSWJR 2-4-0 no. 1335, built by Dübs in 1894. It is about to reverse onto the up line prior to a trip on the Shipston-on-Stour branch. (H.C.Casserley)

──────────▶

13.   When photographed in the 1960s, little had changed in the previous 90 years; even the wide track spacing resulting from the broad gauge era remained. The gaps in the white lines indicated the positions of steps for staff crossing the line. (Lens of Sutton)

14.   The tramway had run across the background of this picture until the coming of the main line. It was diverted along the curved alignment on the right, separating it from its offices and workshops, seen in the left background. (Lens of Sutton)

THE CATHEDRALS EXPRESS

RESTAURANT CAR SERVICE (¶)

LONDON, OXFORD, WORCESTER and HEREFORD

WEEK DAYS

						pm
London (Paddington)	..	..	dep			2A45
Oxford	.. .. ..	..	{	arr		3 56
				dep		4 0
Kingham ..	.. ..	..	..	arr		4 26
Moreton-in-Marsh ..	..	..	„			4 38
Evesham ..	.. ..	..	..	„		4 56
Worcester (Shrub Hill)..		{	arr			5 15
			dep			5 20
Worcester (Foregate Street)..		„				5 25
Malvern Link ..	..	..	..	arr		5 35
Great Malvern	..	..	..	„		5 39
Malvern Wells..	..	..	..	„		5 44
Hereford ..	..	..	..	..	„	6 17

						am
Hereford ..	..	..	..	..	dep	9A50
Ledbury ..	..	..	..	..	„	10 10
Colwall	..	..	..	..	„	10 20
Great Malvern		..	..	..	„	10A27
Malvern Link ..	..	..	..	„		10 31
Worcester (Foregate Street)	{	arr				10 41
		dep				10 42
Worcester (Shrub Hill)..	{	arr				10 45
		dep				10A55
Evesham ..	..	..	..	..	„	11A12
Moreton-in-Marsh ..	..	..	„			11 36
						pm
Oxford	..	..	..	{	arr	12 12
					dep	12 15
Reading General	..	..	{	arr		12 48
				dep		12 50
London (Paddington)	..	..	arr			1 30

A—Seats can be reserved in advance on payment of a fee of 2s. 0d. per seat (see page 23).

¶—Restaurant Car available between London (Paddington) and Worcester (Shrub Hill) in each direction.

November 1959 timetable.

15.   The Shipston branch is included in this record of no. 6922 *Burton Hall* with the "Up Perishables". This would have included much fruit or vegetable traffic from Evesham. (H.F.Wheeller/R.S.Carpenter)

16.   A second photograph from 11th October 1958 and this features a stopping train departing north. Traffic was diminishing, so that two coaches were sufficient. No. 78008 was one of BR's class 2 2-6-0s introduced in 1953. (H.F.Wheeller/R.S.Carpenter)

17.   The 13.30 Hereford to Reading on 6th April 1982 was formed of a second generation DMU, the first having been completely withdrawn in 1962. Note the complexity of the replacement footbridge. (T.Heavyside)

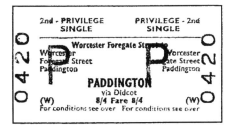

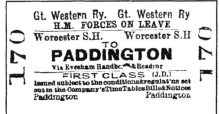

18.　　Most of the sidings had been removed in April 1964, soon after goods traffic had ceased. Having just surrendered the token for the single line in the background, the driver of no. 47806 accelerates the diverted 08.33 Wolverhampton to Poole train on 14th July 1996. (P.G.Barnes)

19.　　The signalman has left his 40-lever signal box on 26th March 2003 and is carrying the token to a train waiting at the down platform. The double track extends towards London for a little over 11 miles. On the right is the washing apron once required for cattle wagons. (V.Mitchell)

20.　　The siding behind the signal box was used occasionally by the track engineers, but on 14th August 2003 it was occupied by newly refurbished no. 165116. The BREL Network Turbos were introduced in 1992. (M.J.Stretton)

Other photographs of this station appear numbered 96 to 106 in the companion album *Oxford to Moreton-in-Marsh*.

ASTON MAGNA SIDING

21.   Aston Magna is two miles north of Moreton-in-Marsh and a siding was laid on the down side in 1902 to serve a brickworks. A "Dean Goods" 0-6-0 is passing on 12th June 1934. (Lens of Sutton coll.)

22.   It seems that the 21-lever signal box was out of use from 1910 to 1920 and closed permanently on 15th December 1946. The siding lasted until March 1957. (Lens of Sutton coll.)

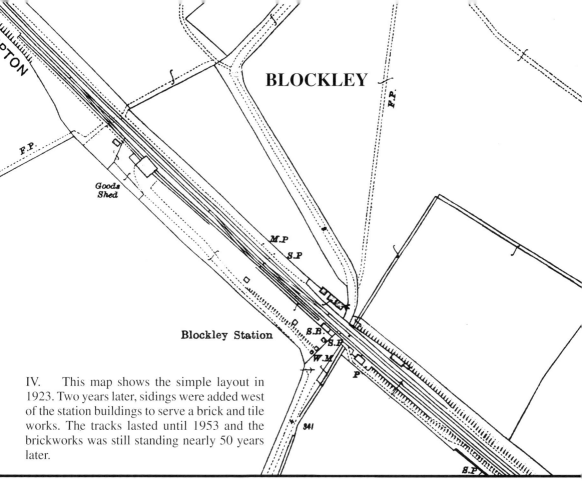

BLOCKLEY

Goods Shed

Blockley Station

IV.   This map shows the simple layout in 1923. Two years later, sidings were added west of the station buildings to serve a brick and tile works. The tracks lasted until 1953 and the brickworks was still standing nearly 50 years later.

23.   This early postcard features the 1918 signal box, which had 25 levers and lasted until 1977. For its final six years, it simply controlled the gates. There was a staff of six for most of the 1920s and 30s. The original timber buildings were replaced in the 1920s. (Lens of Sutton)

24.   The station was 1½ miles from the village, which had a population of about 2400 when passenger service was withdrawn on 3rd January 1966. The structures were photographed in 1952 and freight traffic ceased on 12th July 1964, staffing having ceased on 1st July 1963. (LGRP/NRM)

Blockley	1903	1913	1923	1933
Passenger tickets issued	10146	10901	12705	10803
Season tickets issued	*	*	72	25
Parcels forwarded	9857	9035	6079	5206
General goods forwarded (tons)	1486	2379	1760	76
Coal and coke received (tons)	61	209	108	47
Other minerals received (tons)	1129	1650	1483	1964
General goods received (tons)	1644	1477	1204	699
Trucks of livestock handled	39	45	32	13

(* not available.)

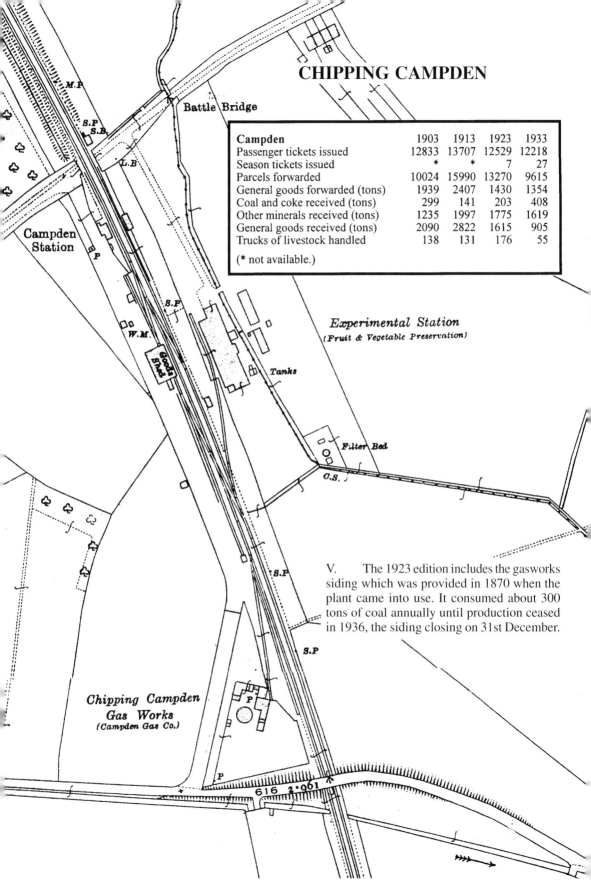

CHIPPING CAMPDEN

Battle Bridge

Campden
Station

Campden	1903	1913	1923	1933
Passenger tickets issued	12833	13707	12529	12218
Season tickets issued	*	*	7	27
Parcels forwarded	10024	15990	13270	9615
General goods forwarded (tons)	1939	2407	1430	1354
Coal and coke received (tons)	299	141	203	408
Other minerals received (tons)	1235	1997	1775	1619
General goods received (tons)	2090	2822	1615	905
Trucks of livestock handled	138	131	176	55

(* not available.)

Experimental Station
(Fruit & Vegetable Preservation)

W.M.

Goods Shed

Tanks

Filter Bed

O.S.

V.   The 1923 edition includes the gasworks
siding which was provided in 1870 when the
plant came into use. It consumed about 300
tons of coal annually until production ceased
in 1936, the siding closing on 31st December.

S.P

Chipping Campden
Gas Works
(Campden Gas Co.)

616 2·961

25. A southward view from the signal box includes the goods shed (right of centre) and vans standing on the left at the factory. This had a siding from 1911 until 1959. (Lens of Sutton)

26. Steam railmotor no. 69 was built in 1906 and by 1912 there were four such units allocated to Worcester. They operated local services between there and Stratford-upon-Avon via Honeybourne or to Moreton-in-Marsh. The buildings are the original OWWR structures. (Lens of Sutton)

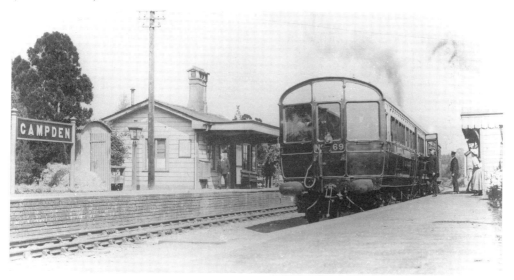

27.	The second coach is on the level crossing as no. 3385 *Newport* departs for Worcester with a stopping train on 11th July 1925. Tapered signal posts give style to the flanks of the picture; no dull tubular posts then. (H.G.W.Household/NRM)

28.	The goods shed housed a 30cwt crane and was photographed in July 1963 in which month freight traffic ceased here. The station had a staff of eleven in 1903, but only six in the 1930s. (R.M.Casserley)

29.   The station had been named simply "Campden" until February 1952. The crossing gates were on the B4035 and were replaced by full lifting barriers in August 1972. Passenger service was withdrawn on 3rd January 1966. (R.M.Casserley)

30.   The signal box was from prior to 1884 and had a new 34-lever frame fitted in 1911. It ceased to be a block post in September 1971 and became a crossing ground frame until closure in July 1978. (D.Lawrence)

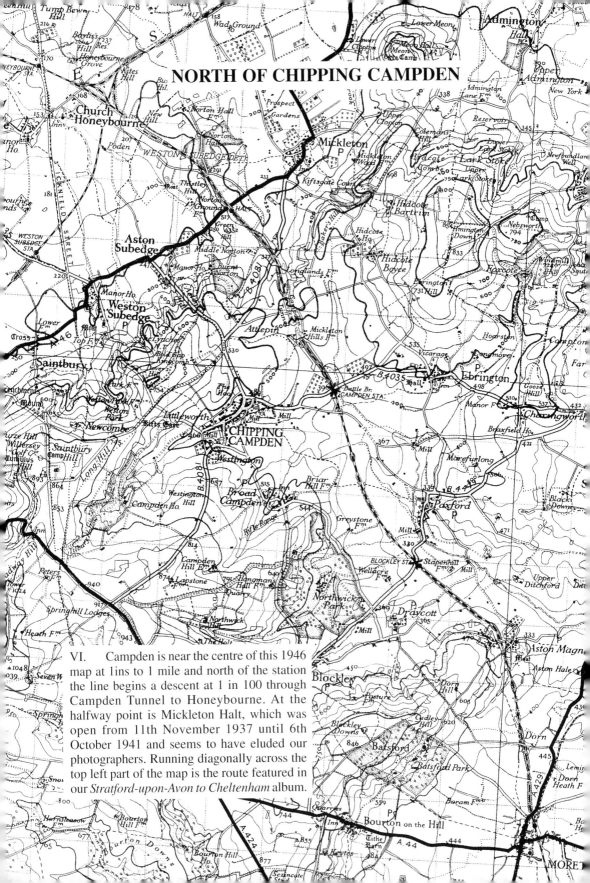

NORTH OF CHIPPING CAMPDEN

VI.   Campden is near the centre of this 1946 map at 1ins to 1 mile and north of the station the line begins a descent at 1 in 100 through Campden Tunnel to Honeybourne. At the halfway point is Mickleton Halt, which was open from 11th November 1937 until 6th October 1941 and seems to have eluded our photographers. Running diagonally across the top left part of the map is the route featured in our *Stratford-upon-Avon to Cheltenham* album.

The Battle of Mickleton

The OWWR was closely associated during its formative years with the GWR, but relations turned sour prior to the protracted construction period. Sir Morton Peto was a key figure in the main contracting firm and by July 1851 a Mr. Marchant was the only partner remaining in the firm of sub-contractors building Campden Tunnel, very slowly. The delays were largely due to lethargic payments by the cash-starved OWWR.

Peto decided to take over the site and Marchant's equipment by force, but was unsuccessful. The OWWR's engineer, I.K.Brunel, arrived with about 300 men on Friday 20th July 1851 to find around 100 of Marchant's workers well armed and the county magistrate in attendance. He advised Brunel not to fight and to leave the site.

Next day, Brunel returned with his gang, assuming that the magistrate would not be present on a Saturday. However, he had returned with a large number of policemen carrying cutlasses and had read the Riot Act to Marchant's force and proceeded to do the same to Brunel's. The latter withdrew.

Brunel broke the Sabbath by ordering gangs to travel from other construction sites. At around 3am on Monday morning he advanced with a total of over 500 navvies and overwhelmed Marchant, despite his pistol. Ugly encounters continued and estimates put Brunel's manpower eventually at 2000. Fighting continued until about 4pm, by which time the police were supported by the Gloucestershire Artillery.

Marchant lost his contract and equipment, Peto lost his reputation and Brunel lost his patience, resigning as engineer to the OWWR in March 1852. Mickleton became a name carved in railway history, but it was not used subsequently, (except for a halt briefly); the tunnel was named after Campden.

Out of favour with the GWR, the OWWR arranged for its London service to be provided by the LNWR from Euston. The initials were subsequently interpreted by many as The "Old Worse & Worse."

31.   The location is given as "Approaching Campden Tunnel", but the locomotive details were not recorded, neither was the date. The photograph was probably taken in 1903, when there was a prolonged period of single line working through the 887yd long tunnel. The engine is an 0-6-0 converted from a 2-2-2 of the "Sir Daniel" class. (P.Q.Treloar coll.)

32. No details were kept of this up freight on Campden Bank in icy conditions. No doubt the sweat was dropping from the fireman during the stiff four-mile climb at 1 in 100. DMU's now usually maintain 70mph on this incline. (D.Lawrence)

VII. The location of this 1923 map (at 20ins to 1 mile) can be seen top left on the previous one. The signal box lower right is West Loop; it was in use from 1904 until 1960. Beyond the right border was South Loop Junction (1907-65. 23 levers). On the left page is North Loop Junction (1904-33. 31 levers). The lines continue on the right of the next map. The dates of South Loop were 1907-65, North Loop (Cheltenham & Honeybourne on the map) 1904-81. The Hatton & Honeybourne Curve (East Loop) was closed from 1970 to 1981. It was reopened to give a direct line northwards to Long Marston. Three tip sidings were laid south of North Loop in 1960 and were in use, mainly for spent ballast, until 1996.

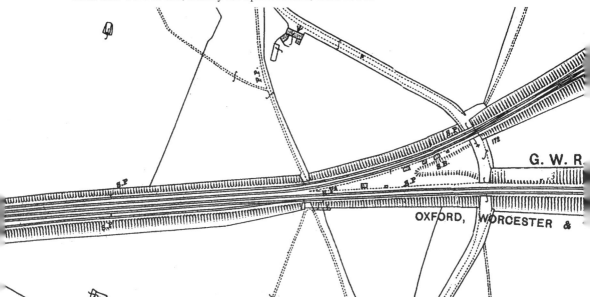

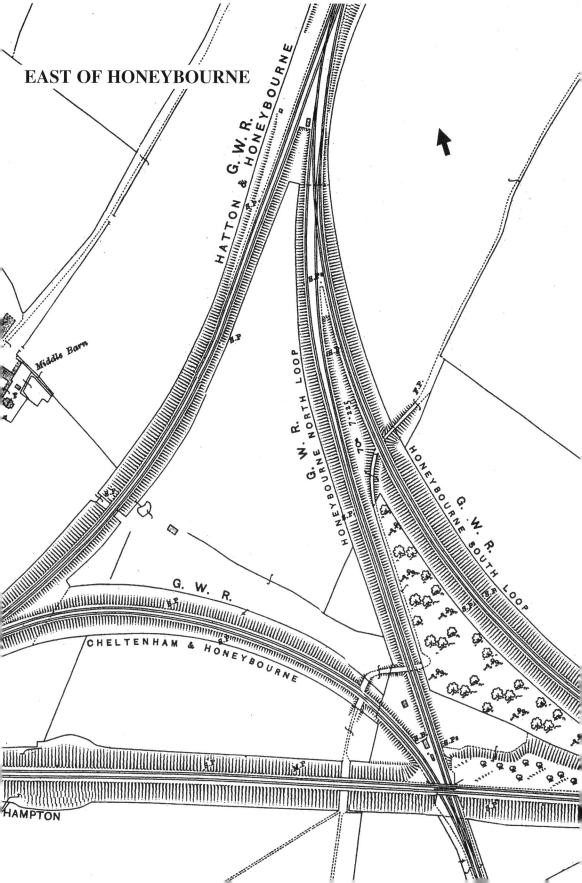

EAST OF HONEYBOURNE

Middle Barn

HATTON & G. W. R. HONEYBOURNE

G. W. R. NORTH LOOP

HONEYBOURNE

7·25

70

HONEYBOURNE G. W. R. SOUTH LOOP

G. W. R.

CHELTENHAM & HONEYBOURNE

HAMPTON

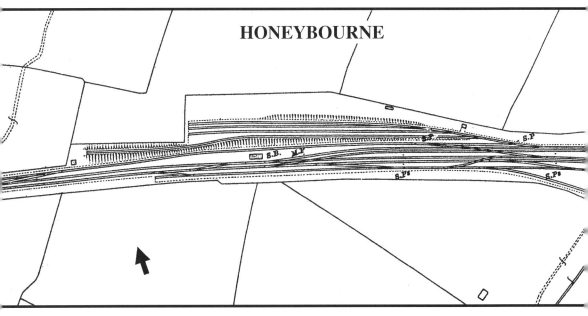

HONEYBOURNE

33.   An eastward panorama from the road bridge features Station South Box (1909-83. 57 levers), which was an unstaffed ground frame with only 21 levers after 1971. Station North Box (1909-65. 62 levers) is shown on the left page of the map. (Lens of Sutton coll.)

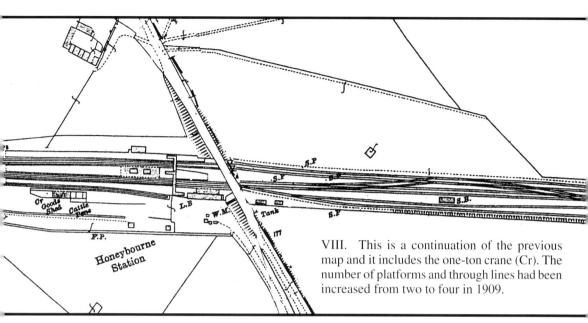

VIII. This is a continuation of the previous map and it includes the one-ton crane (Cr). The number of platforms and through lines had been increased from two to four in 1909.

34. Main line trains pass at platforms 1 and 2, while a connecting service stands at no. 3. The number of milk churns suggest that this is prior to about 1930, when bulk tankers began to be introduced. (Lens of Sutton)

35.   Two photographs from about 1933 both include parts of the goods shed roof. Local goods traffic was concentrated south of the main line and it ceased on 1st January 1964. Six more sidings were added on the down side in 1942, but they had gone by 1964. (Brunel University/Mowat coll.)

36.   The 1909 reconstruction was undertaken using standard GWR building plans and an inspection pit was provided in the right foreground. Staffing levels ranged from 11 in 1903, to 40 in 1923 and 31 in 1933. (Brunel University/Mowat coll.)

37.   The main building on the right included a refreshment room for many years. The connections allowed trains from the north-south route to use any of the platforms. The bridge span on the left dates from 1909. (Lens of Sutton)

38.   Assorted vans are in tow as no. 4997 *Elton Hall* creeps into platform 2 on 7th March 1959, having passed an adverse distant signal. The train will have passed the massive Sheen Hill Depot, which was a government store in use from 1943 to 1963. It was one mile from the station, on the up side, and there was a 30-lever signal box from 1943 to 1951. (R.M.Casserley)

→

39.   The GWR had consideration for its passengers: a fully glazed footbridge, a trussed roof that did not require stanchions near the building and a massive screen for the doorway to the gentlemens. (D.Lawrence)

40.   An autocoach was often provided for the Cheltenham stopping service and 0-4-2T no. 1424 was typical of the motive power. Such trains were withdrawn in 1960, but the route remained usable until 1976. (D.Lawrence)

41.   It was possible to travel from here to Stratford-upon-Avon from 1859, but there was a wait until 1908 for the first train to Cheltenham. It was this extra traffic that prompted the rebuild. (Lens of Sutton)

Honeybourne	1903	1913	1923	1933
Passenger tickets issued	17282	15119	18210	13862
Season tickets issued	*	*	53	67
Parcels forwarded	5961	7733	6789	2555
General goods forwarded (tons)	2471	1268	589	522
Coal and coke received (tons)	254	43	11	134
Other minerals received (tons)	23598	447	470	1538
General goods received (tons)	10615	581	638	301
Trucks of livestock handled	142	209	161	170

(* not available.)

42.   Our last view of steam at this location features class 9F 2-10-0 no. 92235. The other engine is near the site of a locomotive shed that was demolished in 1907. Passenger service here ended on 5th May 1969, when the Birmingham service ceased. (M.J.Stretton coll.)

For details of the lines north and south, please see our
Stratford-upon-Avon to Cheltenham **album.**

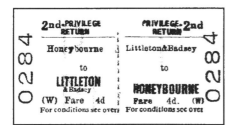

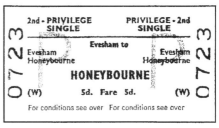

43.   Trains called again from 22nd May 1981, but only a bus shelter was provided. This eastward view is from March 2003 and includes the Long Marston connection. There was a loop in the grass on the left and there were three rarely-used sidings to the west of it. (V.Mitchell)

44.   The run-round loop for Long Marston traffic is on the left as we leave for Worcester on the same day. Photographs 117 to 120 feature Long Marston Depot. (V.Mitchell)

LITTLETON AND BADSEY

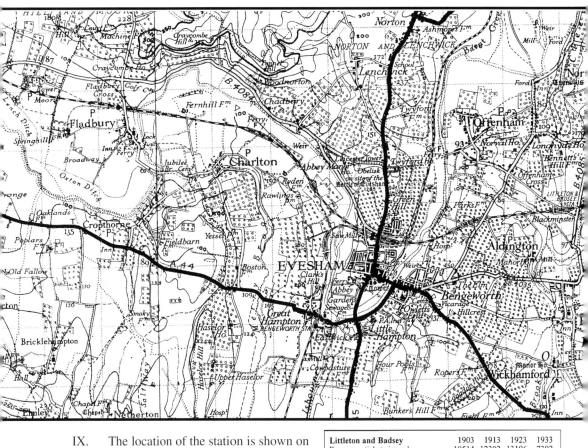

IX.   The location of the station is shown on the right of this 1946 map, which is at 1ins to 1 mile. It also includes the LMS single line from Redditch (top); this passes over our route on its approach to Evesham. The single line continues to Ashchurch beyond the lower border, close to yet more orchards.

Littleton and Badsey	1903	1913	1923	1933
Passenger tickets issued	10514	12302	13196	7392
Season tickets issued	*	*	96	27
Parcels forwarded	2968	7362	36408	15915
General goods forwarded (tons)	4473	6465	7753	7111
Coal and coke received (tons)	68	187	280	372
Other minerals received (tons)	1850	2776	3659	4884
General goods received (tons)	1778	2145	3051	1724
Trucks of livestock handled	-	-	4	-

(* not available.)

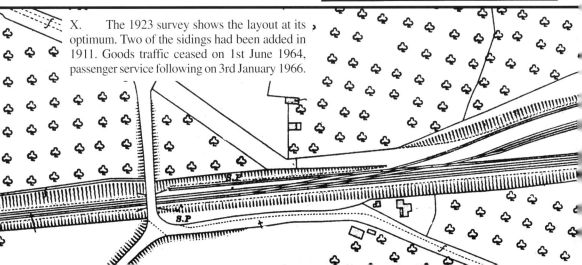

X.   The 1923 survey shows the layout at its optimum. Two of the sidings had been added in 1911. Goods traffic ceased on 1st June 1964, passenger service following on 3rd January 1966.

45.   Shunting is in progress on the up line as no. 4967 *Shirenewton Hall* accelerates an Oxford to Worcester train, sometime in the early 1930s. There was a staff of 12 in that period, this rising to 16 in the late 1930s. (R.S.Carpenter coll.)

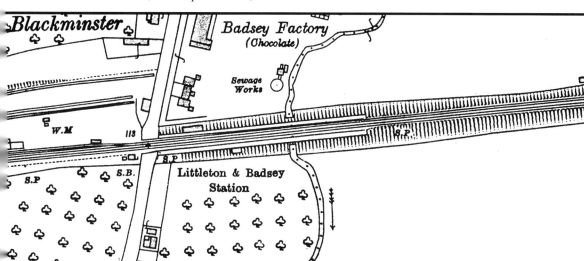

46.   Most OWWR stations were rebuilt in brick; this is thought to be one of the original style. We are looking at the up side from the level crossing in 1960; the gates were replaced by full lifting barriers in 1979. The nearby 1884 signal box had an 18-lever frame installed in 1910. It was in use until 1979, although only controlling the crossing after the singling in 1971. The site is used for car breaking. (P.J.Garland/R.S.Carpenter)

EAST OF EVESHAM

XI.   Aldington Siding was half a mile from Evesham and was in existence by 1882; it was closed in 1959. The 23-lever signal box dated from 1911 and it also lasted until 1959.

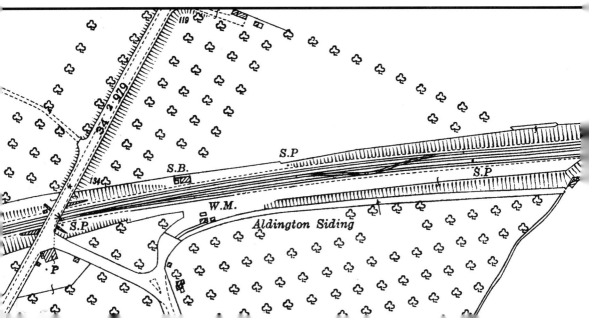

EVESHAM

47.   An early, but indifferent, postcard view gives a rare sight of the goods shed and the inspection pit at the end of the down platform. The locomotive is 4-2-2 *Albert Edward.*
(Lens of Sutton)

48.   The number of employees rose from 36 in 1903 to 68 in 1932, in response to the increase in the fruit and vegetable trade. The gents had a less modest door screen than that at Honeybourne.
(Lens of Sutton)

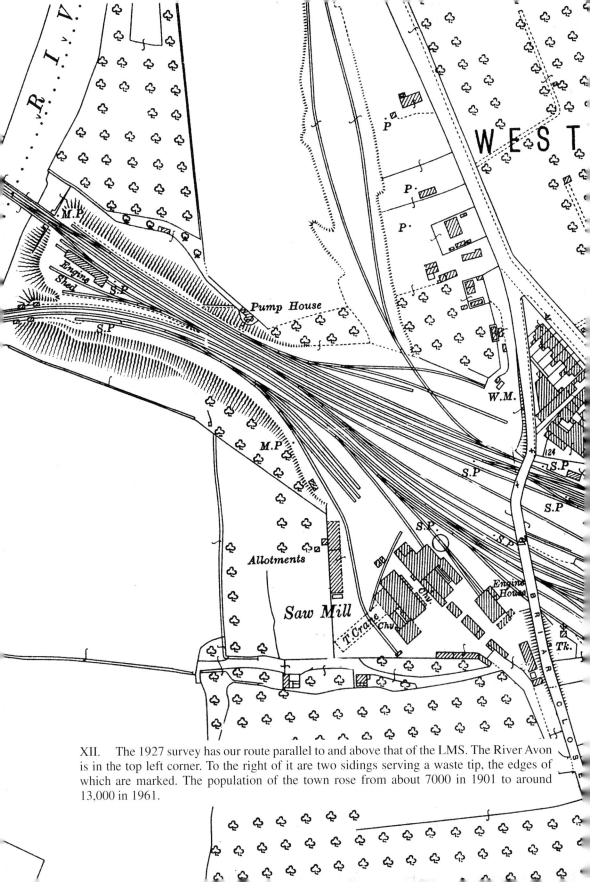

R I V.

M.P

Engine
Shed S.P

S.P

S.P

Pump House

WEST

P.

P.

P.

W.M.

M.P

Allotments

Saw Mill

T. Crane

Chy.

Chy.

Engine
House

124

S.P

S.P

S.P

S.P

S.P

Tk.

XII.   The 1927 survey has our route parallel to and above that of the LMS. The River Avon is in the top left corner. To the right of it are two sidings serving a waste tip, the edges of which are marked. The population of the town rose from about 7000 in 1901 to around 13,000 in 1961.

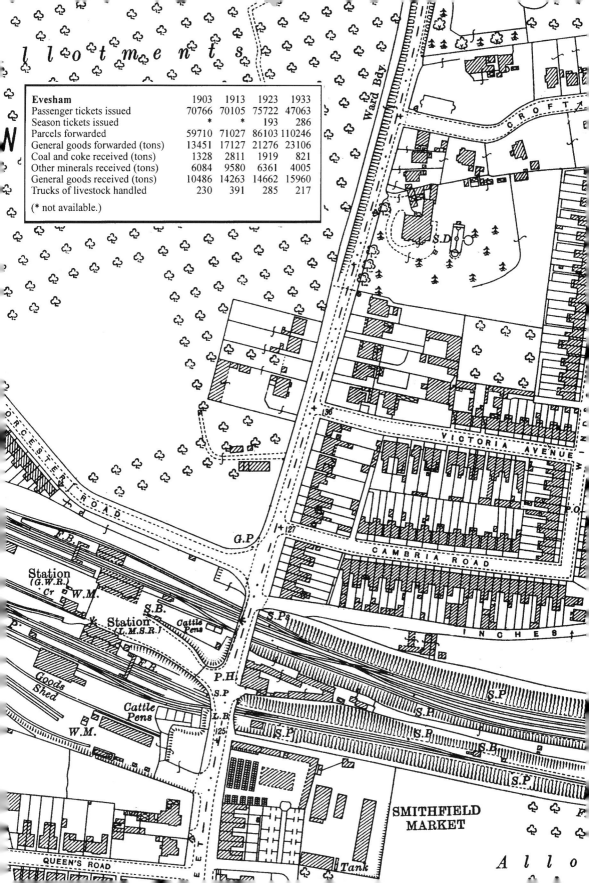

Evesham	1903	1913	1923	1933
Passenger tickets issued	70766	70105	75722	47063
Season tickets issued	*	*	193	286
Parcels forwarded	59710	71027	86103	110246
General goods forwarded (tons)	13451	17127	21276	23106
Coal and coke received (tons)	1328	2811	1919	821
Other minerals received (tons)	6084	9580	6361	4005
General goods received (tons)	10486	14263	14662	15960
Trucks of livestock handled	230	391	285	217

(* not available.)

49.   A westward view from June 1934 includes South Box, which had a 48-lever frame fitted in 1924 and was in use until 1957. North Box was west of the river and appears on the next map. (Brunel University/Mowat coll.)

50.   The 2.0pm from Worcester on 31st July 1937 was carrying H M Queen Mary from Ledbury to London. It was hauled by no. 5063 *Earl Baldwin*. Note the six-wheeled bogies under the Royal Saloon and part of the new goods yard on the right. (R.S.Carpenter coll.)

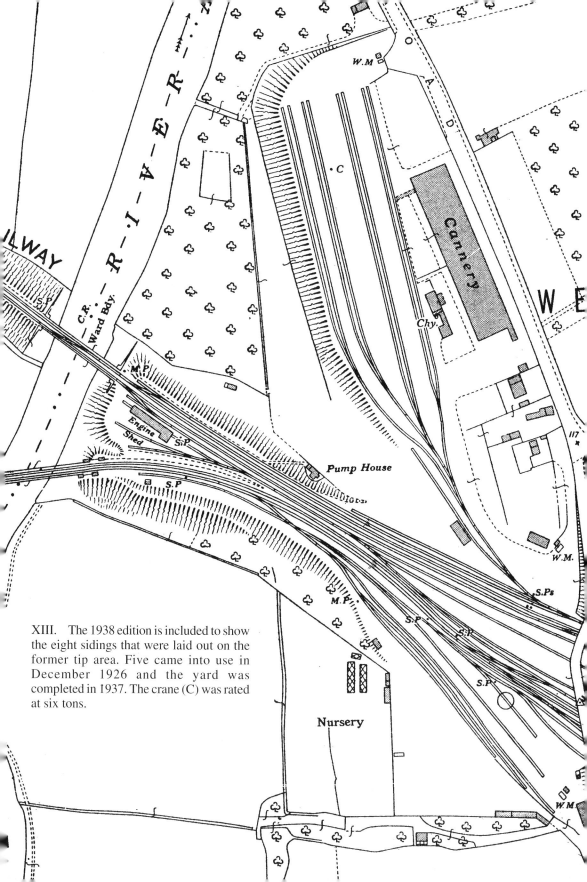

RIVER

ILWAY

S.P

C.R.
Ward Bdy.

W.M

O
A
D

· C

Cannery

W E

Chy.

M.P.

Engine
Shed S.P.

Pump House

S.P

S.P

117

W.M.

S.Ps

M.P.

S.P

S.P

S.P

XIII. The 1938 edition is included to show
the eight sidings that were laid out on the
former tip area. Five came into use in
December 1926 and the yard was
completed in 1937. The crane (C) was rated
at six tons.

Nursery

W.M

51.   The south elevation was recorded in March 1949. The building was largely intact more than 50 years later and continued to have a staffed ticket office. Steam returned to the area in August 2002 when the 15ins gauge Evesham Vale Light Railway began operating about one mile north of the town. (Lens of Sutton)

52.   Looking east in 1955, we see the small brick arch which accommodated the loop line, the platform face for which was shorter than the adjacent one. The line under that arch was removed during the singling of 1971. (N.Simmons)

53.   The ex-LMS building is on the left with the sign for platforms 1 & 2. It was officially "Evesham South" from September 1951. All goods traffic was handled by LMS staff from 1932. The former GWR premises are on the right. (D.Lawrence)

54.   The engine shed was close to the river and was a sub-shed of Worcester. It is seen on 24th April 1955 with two class 9400 0-6-0PTs nearby and the former LMS lines in the foreground. The allocation in 1938 was one 2300 and one 4500, while in 1947 it was just one 2700 class 0-6-0PT. (F.Hornby)

55.   We can now enjoy three photographs from March 1958. A railcar is westbound as no. 5065 *Newport Castle* waits to depart for London. Also visible is the loop line and the hairpin roadway to the up side entrance. (P.Q.Treloar)

56.   No. 9429 approaches with a down local service and passes the loop points. The sidings on the right lasted until 1965; the one on the right was for carriage berthing and the other was a refuge siding for freight trains. In the background is the bridge for the Redditch line. (P.Q.Treloar)

57.   A Cardiff to Birmingham DMU was diverted from its direct route at Ashbourne to run via Honeybourne and Stratford-upon-Avon. It is seen leaving the former LMS route as it approaches platform 4. (P.Q.Treloar)

58.   No. 5952 *Cogan Hall* is about to leave with a semi-fast down train, sometime in July 1959. The goods shed doorway appears to have been designed for broad gauge stock. Staff accommodation is on the left. (RAS Marketing)

59.   The engine shed (left) closed in June 1961 and the new signal box (above the trains) came into use on 9th March 1957. No. 3840 is passing a DMU standing on the up goods line in October 1962. (RAS Marketing)

60.   A terminating DMU stands in the "Cripple Siding" on 14th November 1963, as a 5700 class 0-6-0PT departs west with empty wagons. A BR container is next to the brake van. (J.M.Tolson/F.Hornby)

61.   The footbridge had recently lost its roof when no. 6910 *Gossington Hall* was captured on film with the 1.25pm Oxford to Worcester on 13th July 1963. (R.M.Casserley)

62.   The line to Ashchurch had been in the foreground until its closure in 1963. No. 50018 *Resolution* is working the 16.03 Worcester to Paddington service on 6th April 1982. The goods yard was taken out of use in 1981. (T.Heavyside)

63.   From the other side of the same bridge, we observe a DMU from Oxford departing on 16th February 1985. Part of the former loop was still in place about 20 years later. (T.Heavyside)

64.   This 1996 panorama confirms that most of the buildings were intact and the picture includes the connection to the engineers sidings. There had been an engine shed to the right of the camera until 1901. Upon arrival, guards of down trains have to telephone the signal box to advise that the train has arrived complete. (P.G.Barnes)

65. The diverted 10.50 Manchester Piccadilly to Southampton HST is leaving the single track on 14th July 1996. The sidings on the right were retained by the engineers. (P.G.Barnes)

66. The 1957 signal box was fitted with a 72-lever frame. The foot crossing in front of it was used for the transfer of the electric tokens for the sections to Worcester and to Moreton-in-Marsh. This photograph is from the rear of a departing train in 2003; it seems strange that a 19th century single line system was installed here in the late 20th century. (V.Mitchell)

67.   An eastward view in 2003 includes one abutment of the bridge first used by MR trains and also the 75mph speed restriction sign. The points were electrically operated, but the signal was mechanically controlled. (V.Mitchell)

68.   The up starting signal was one of the few centre pivot ones remaining in use and is on the down side. Also included is the 10-car stop sign for HST drivers. (P.G.Barnes)

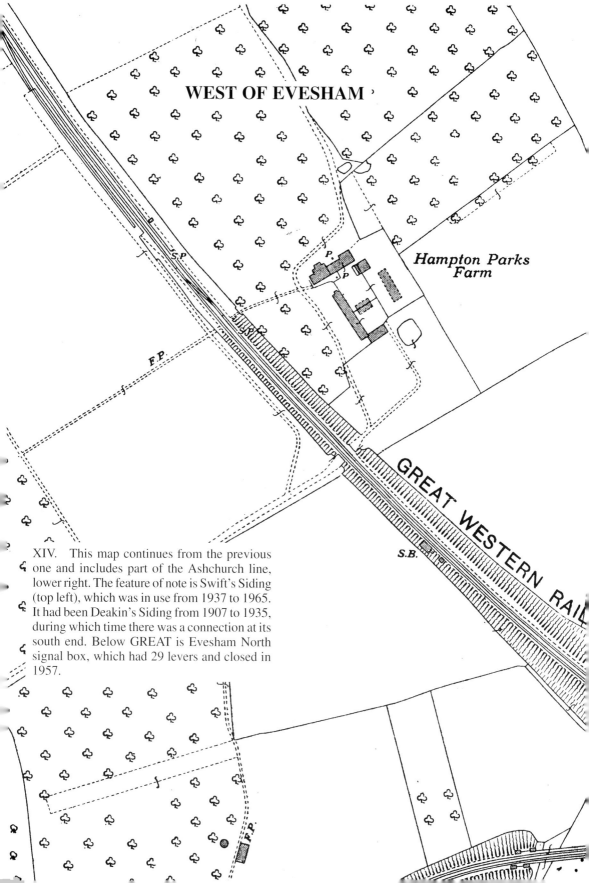

WEST OF EVESHAM

Hampton Parks Farm

S.P.

F.P.

F.P.

S.B.

GREAT WESTERN RAIL

XIV. This map continues from the previous one and includes part of the Ashchurch line, lower right. The feature of note is Swift's Siding (top left), which was in use from 1937 to 1965. It had been Deakin's Siding from 1907 to 1935, during which time there was a connection at its south end. Below GREAT is Evesham North signal box, which had 29 levers and closed in 1957.

69.   The rivetted lattice structure over the River Avon was recorded on 14th July 1996 as the diverted 11.15 Poole to Manchester Piccadilly accelerated westwards. (P.G.Barnes)

XV.   Two miles from the bridge, there was a public goods depot known as Charlton Siding. It is shown on the 1927 edition and was in use until 11th August 1963, when the signal box (right) closed. This had been completed in 1902 and had 19 levers.

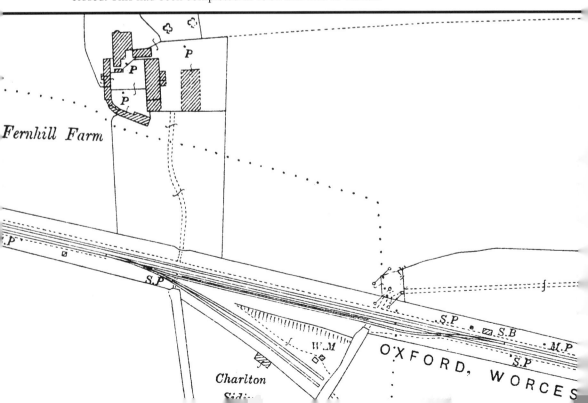

Fernhill Farm

Charlton
Sid

OXFORD, WORCES

FLADBURY

70.   There was limited local traffic as the population was only 467 in 1901 and about 600 at the time of closure. There was a staff of seven for most of the 1930s. (Lens of Sutton coll.)

71.   A westward panorama from 1962 includes the office for the weighbridge on the left and an uncommon type of waiting room on the right. Goods traffic ceased on 1st July 1963 and the 22-lever signal box closed on 13th September 1964. (Brunel University/Mowat coll.)

Fladbury	1903	1913	1923	1933
Passenger tickets issued	20343	21039	23692	22975
Season tickets issued	*	*	35	51
Parcels forwarded	11513	6901	5879	4013
General goods forwarded (tons)	3705	4588	5234	4728
Coal and coke received (tons)	61	16	65	982
Other minerals received (tons)	2772	2569	1233	2125
General goods received (tons)	1746	2090	2078	961
Trucks of livestock handled	13	21	26	70

(* not available.)

XVI. The 1927 map shows the layout at its optimum. The gate on the private siding was at the boundary of the pages. The loop to the left of it was provided in 1924.

XVII. The extent of the branch is shown on the left of map IX. This line to Bomford's Spring Mill Farm was in use from 1879 to 1963. It continues from the map above, albeit with a gap.

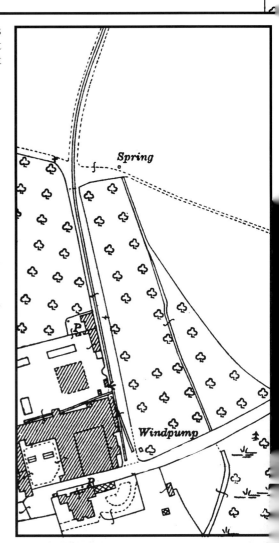

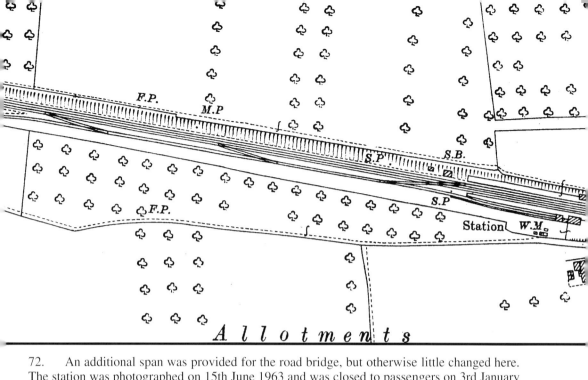

72.   An additional span was provided for the road bridge, but otherwise little changed here. The station was photographed on 15th June 1963 and was closed to passengers on 3rd January 1966. (R.M.Casserley)

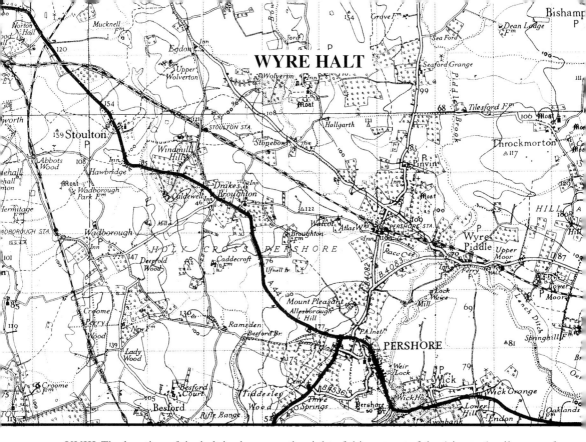

XVIII. The location of the halt is shown on the right of this extract of the 1 ins to 1 mile map of 1946. Norton Junction is on the left.

73.   The halt opened on 11th June 1934 and was situated south of the B4083 at Wyre Piddle. This view towards Worcester is from 26th April 1958. Closure took place on 3rd January 1966. (R.M.Casserley)

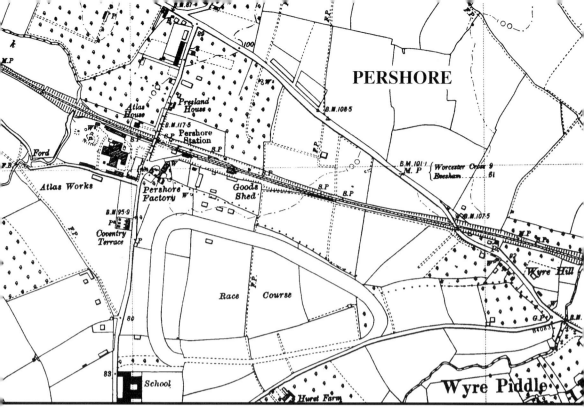

XIX. The 1938 survey at 6 ins to 1 mile shows the close proximity of the racecourse and includes yet more orchards. The Atlas Works produced agricultural implements.

74.   A westward postcard view shows the GWR's enhancements, but the unusual building on the right may be of OWWR origin. There were 18 or 19 employees in the 1930s.
(Lens of Sutton coll.)

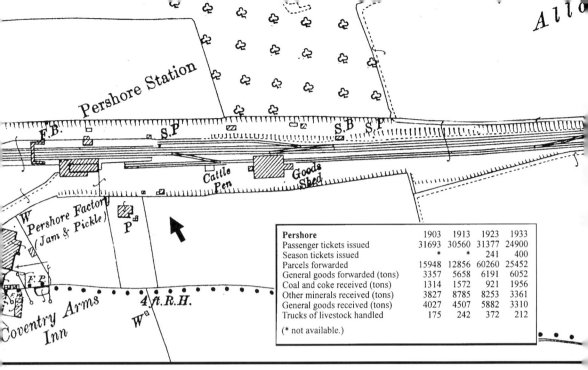

Pershore	1903	1913	1923	1933
Passenger tickets issued	31693	30560	31377	24900
Season tickets issued	*	*	241	400
Parcels forwarded	15948	12856	60260	25452
General goods forwarded (tons)	3357	5658	6191	6052
Coal and coke received (tons)	1314	1572	921	1956
Other minerals received (tons)	3827	8785	8253	3361
General goods received (tons)	4027	4507	5882	3310
Trucks of livestock handled	175	242	372	212

(* not available.)

XX.   The 1904 edition shows an arrangement that existed from 1872 to 1912, when a siding for a horse loading dock and a loop were laid north of the up platform. The station is about one mile north of the town centre.

75.   The loop points are included, as is the 1924 siding extension. A second parallel siding was added at an unknown date. This and the next photograph are from the early 1950s. The population rose from 3348 in 1901 to 5181 in 1961. (J.H.Moss/R.S.Carpenter)

76.   The signal box had 44 levers and was in use from 26th April 1936 (when the loop was extended eastwards) until 18th September 1968. Also visible is the six-ton crane. Fruit was the main commodity despatched in July and August, while vegetables were handled from November to June. Plums were a local speciality, about 70 wagons being loaded daily in season. (J.H.Moss/R.S.Carpenter)

77.   No. 6849 *Walton Grange* stands near the parcels shelter, not long before the end of steam. Back in the Summer of 1939, up to 21 non-passenger trains were scheduled to call, 12 of them running "as required". (D.Lawrence)

78.   We now have three photographs from 3rd May 1969. From 5th May, Pershore was given its worst ever train service: one up and one down, weekdays only. The latter was the 07.14 Moreton-in-Marsh to Hereford, calling at 08.14. (D.Johnson/Millbrook House)

79.   In the reverse direction, there was a train at 17.54, which terminated at the next station. This awful timetable lasted until 1976. However, two trains were added in 1975, but not advertised in timetables! Condemned coaches stand in the one remaining siding. Goods traffic had ceased on 2nd November 1964. (D.Johnson/Millbrook House)

NOTICE TO TRACTION ENGINE DRIVERS

WHEELS OF TRACTION ENGINES NOT TO APPROACH WITHIN 6 FEET OF OUTER EDGE OF WHARF WALL COPING

80. A remarkable link with the past survived in the form of this warning. Much older is the post on which it is mounted; we are looking at the underside of a bridge rail from broad gauge track. (D.Johnson/Millbrook House)

81. The goods office and the west elevation are seen from the loading dock, which was the scene of hectic activity in the fruit and veg seasons. The foot crossing gave access to the up yard. (J.H.Moss/R.S.Carpenter)

82.   This view is in the same direction as the previous one. The fireplace is beyond the desk on the left. The office was lit by gas until 1939, but clerks had to continue to stand at their work. (J.H.Moss)

83.   Demolition of the buildings had begun when this photograph was taken in March 1970. The buffers on the left arrived in October 1965, when the goods loop was truncated. Paradoxically, the site is now used to produce road dressings. (D.J.Hyde)

84.   Unfortunately, the track retained in the 1971 singling had the oldest material. Seen on it on 6th April 1982 is the 16.48 Hereford to Oxford DMU. (T.Heavyside)

85.   The arrival of two more shelters by the time that this photograph was taken in 2003 reflects the increase in traffic. Part of the former up platform was still in place. The running-in nameboard was provided by the Cotswold Line Promotion Group. (V.Mitchell)

STOULTON

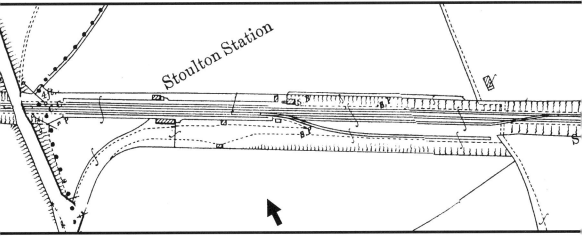

XXI. The map is from 1904 and shows a track arrangement that was never altered. The station, goods yard and 22-lever signal box all opened on 20th February 1899. The village housed about 400 souls at that time.

Stoulton	1903	1913	1923	1933
Passenger tickets issued	5879	4575	3932	2430
Season tickets issued	*	*	24	13
Parcels forwarded	1277	2582	2838	1585
General goods forwarded (tons)	469	495	358	375
Coal and coke received (tons)	6	44	-	77
Other minerals received (tons)	1212	535	3671	75
General goods received (tons)	159	182	183	137
Trucks of livestock handled	-	-	-	-
(* not available.)				

86.   No. 7025 *Sudeley Castle* heads a down express and passes a wagon in the small goods yard, which closed on 1st July 1963. There were normally two men here, but only one after 1957. The signal box closed on 19th April 1964 and passenger service was withdrawn on 3rd January 1966. The photo date is 15th June 1963. (D.Johnson/Millbrook House)

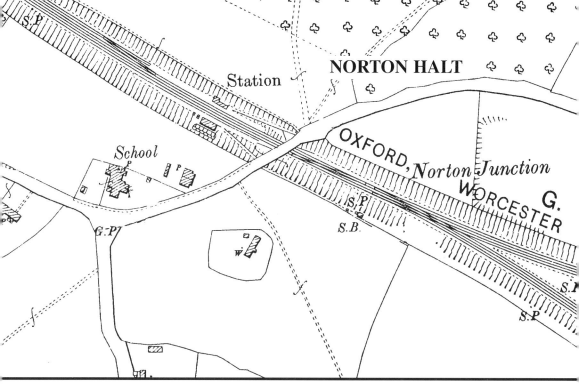

XXII. The location of the station is at the extreme left of map XVIII. This is the 1904 survey and includes the inclined footways leading down to the platforms. Opening took place on 5th October 1850, only MR trains using it for the first two years. There was just a single line initially.

87. Although termed "Norton Junction", trains from the Gloucester route seldom stopped here, except in the initial years. Note the tall chimney pots, used owing to down-draught in the cutting. (Lens of Sutton)

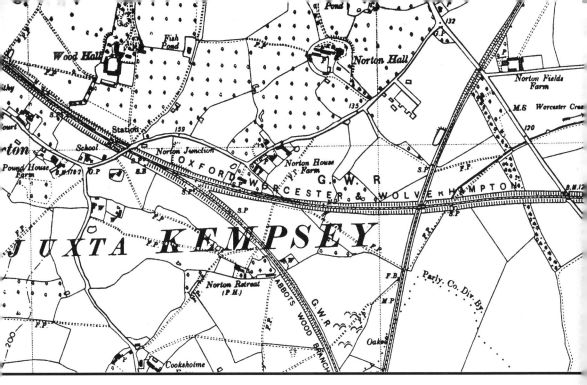

XXIII. The 1938 survey at 6 ins to 1 mile has the station's solitary goods siding below the word WORCESTER. It was a loop line until 1959.

88.   The points to the up refuge siding are on the left. The other siding was used for goods traffic until 1st July 1963. Back in 1895, there were five down trains calling here.
(Lens of Sutton coll.)

89.   There were five or six employed here during the first 40 years of the 20th century and by 1922 there were still only five trains stopping, weekdays only. (Lens of Sutton coll.)

90.   Staffing ceased on 7th September 1959 and "Norton Junction" became "Norton Halt". Closure took place on 3rd January 1966, by which time the service had increased to eight trains in the down direction. (D.Lawrence)

91.   No. B428 takes to the Evesham line on 27th April 1984, while working a Worcester to Oxford service. Although there is a walkway for the signaller, the electric tablet operation is usually done in a machine on the platform at Worcester. (T.Heavyside)

92.   The signal box was still in use in 2003 and was photographed from a train from Oxford that had just used the crossover. The box was fitted with a 33-lever frame. (V.Mitchell)

SOUTH OF WORCESTER

XXIV. This 1888 extract has our route at the bottom. Whilst the station was a joint one, the GWR and MR had separate engine sheds. The map continues at the bottom of the next one.

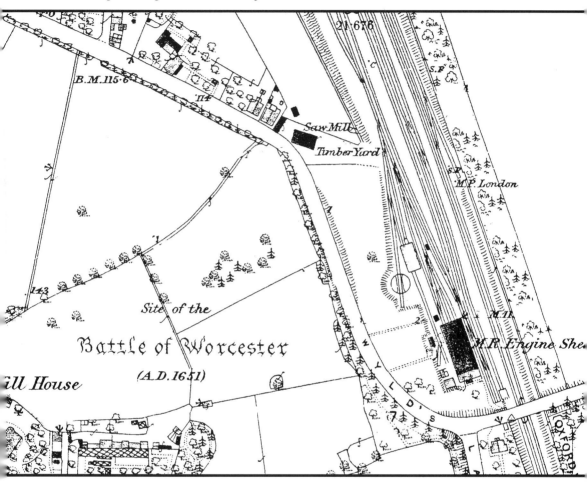

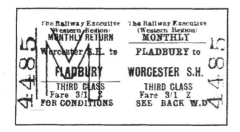

93.   A smartly groomed "Castle" accelerates an up "Cathedrals Express" near the goods shed marked on the next map. Behind the camera is Wyld's Lane signal box, which had 41 levers and lasted until September 1973. (W.J.Probert/Millbrook House)

94.   To the right of the previous camera position was this water tank, which was at the south end of the marshalling yard. Ex-GWR 0-6-0 no. 2207 is on the through goods line on 18th March 1960. (P.Q.Treloar coll.)

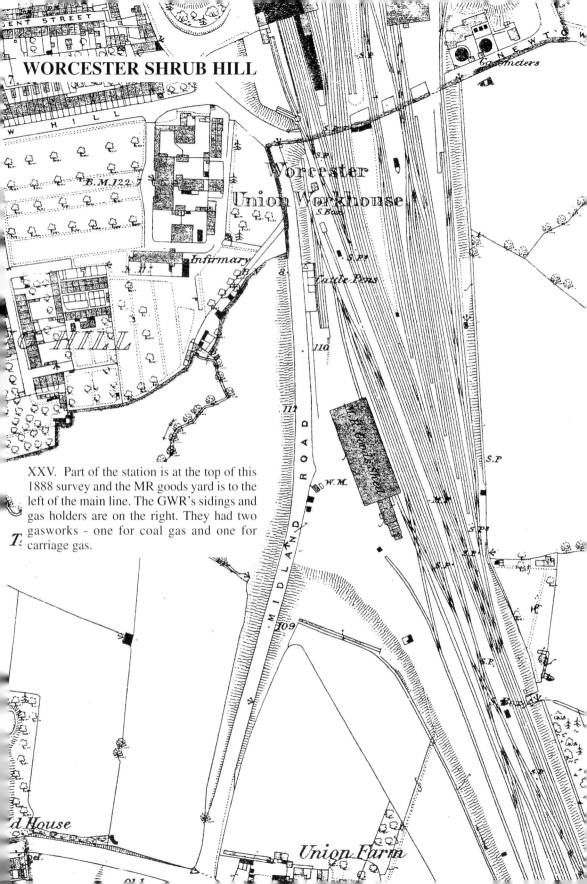

WORCESTER SHRUB HILL

XXV. Part of the station is at the top of this 1888 survey and the MR goods yard is to the left of the main line. The GWR's sidings and gas holders are on the right. They had two gasworks - one for coal gas and one for carriage gas.

95.   The joint station was provided with four through tracks, but only two platforms under the main span. The lattice footbridge begins near the sign GENTLEMEN FIRST CLASS. This is a northward view in about 1910. (Lens of Sutton coll.)

96.   The north elevation is featured, along with both footbridges and the additional two-road train shed. The centre tracks were provided with scissors crossovers to the platform lines, this aiding the joining and splitting of trains. (Lens of Sutton)

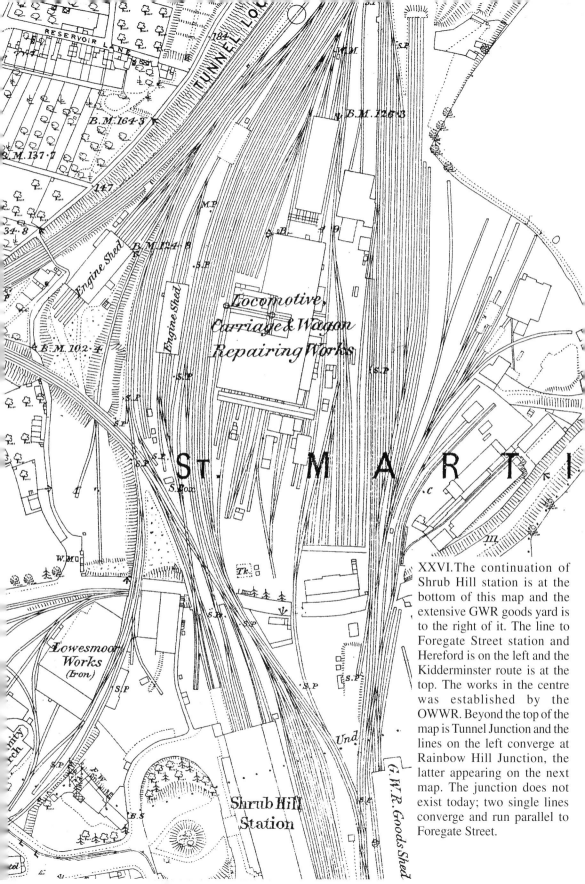

RESERVOIR LANE

TUNNEL LO

B.M.164·3

B.M.137·7

147

34·8

B.M.124·8

Engine Shed

M.P.

S.B.

B.M.126·3

S.P.

Engine Shed

Locomotive,
Carriage & Wagon
Repairing Works

S.P.

B.M.102·4

S.P.

S.P.

S.P.

S.B.

S.P.

S.Box

ST. MARTI

.c

III

W.M.

Tk.

Sh.

S.P.

Lowesmoor
Works
(Iron)

S.P.

S.P.

S.P.

S.P.

Und.

G.W.R. Goods Shed

S.P.

rch

B.S

Shrub Hill
Station

XXVI. The continuation of Shrub Hill station is at the bottom of this map and the extensive GWR goods yard is to the right of it. The line to Foregate Street station and Hereford is on the left and the Kidderminster route is at the top. The works in the centre was established by the OWWR. Beyond the top of the map is Tunnel Junction and the lines on the left converge at Rainbow Hill Junction, the latter appearing on the next map. The junction does not exist today; two single lines converge and run parallel to Foregate Street.

97. A 1934 view of the south end includes Joint Station signal box, which had 61 levers and closed in the following year. There is a single crossover between the central tracks in front of the "Prairie" 2-6-2T (Brunel University/Mowat coll.)

98. A rare photograph from 1943 reveals office conditions in that period. The 1938 staff records show 75 engaged on the passenger side and 135 on goods traffic. The front three men have small telephone exchanges on their desks. (Brunel University/Clinker coll.)

XXVII. The right of this map continues from the left of the previous two and includes part of the city's street tramway, plus the 1872 branch to the Worcester Vinegar Works (lower centre). The Worcester & Birmingham Canal runs from top to bottom and the gasworks was built alongside it in 1818. By 1900, it was consuming 22,000 tons of coal per annum, this peaking at 52,768 in 1943. The works declined in stages in the mid-1960s. Its siding passes through the West Central Wagon Works, as do those from the main part of the Vulcan Works. Reference to the previous map will show that all traffic to and from all these premises passed over the main lines on the level. To the left of the crossings are the two sidings of a coal yard, access to which was *under* the main lines.

99.   This is the north end on 30th April 1956, with 2-6-2T no. 4553 in attendance. The main roof had been removed by 1940 and the other had followed later. (H.C.Casserley)

100.   No. 4088 *Dartmouth Castle* leaves for London and passes 0-6-0PT no. 4680, sometime in the early 1960s. The train on the right is probably bound for Gloucester or beyond. (Millbrook House)

101.	Before entering the Vinegar Works, the line passed over Pheasant Street. This unique three armed signal was in use until 1939, and, like the branch, was maintained by the GWR. There was a curious four-way lantern on the post. In the background are the offices of the Vulcan Works, which housed McKenzie & Holland, railway signal engineers.
(GWR Magazine)

102.	The	12.25pm	to Leamington Spa was recorded departing on 27th December 1960. No. 6133 would run via Honeybourne and Stratford-upon-Avon and arrive at 2.14pm.
(Millbrook House)

103.   Seen from the base of the signal box on 10th March 1961 are no. 7004 *Eastnor Castle* with the 12.55pm Worcester to Paddington, no. 6975 *Capesthorne Hall* with the 12.25 to Leamington Spa and no. 45629 *Straits Settlements* heading the 12.20 to Gloucester Eastgate. (Millbrook House)

104.   The elevated position of the station is evident and this picture explains why the street tramway shown on map XXVI terminated in the foreground. The siding crossing the tramway near the word HILL ran to the Vinegar Works of Hill, Evans & Co. This and the next picture are from September 1964. (H.C.Casserley)

105. The nearer of the two signals appears in the previous picture. They were for the benefit of road users. Behind the car on the right is a level crossing over which trains on the Lowesmoor Tramway passed to and from the Vinegar Works. An 0-6-0PT was liable to emerge from a gap in the wall until 5th June 1964. (H.C.Casserley)

106. A northward panorama from July 1967 includes (on the left) the 72-lever Junction box, which was in use until November 1973. There are two engine sheds on the left and the former locoworks is on the right. (H.C.Casserley)

107. No. 31254 stands at the rear of the 13.09 from Paddington on 15th September 1975 and is about to remove the empty stock. The white edged canopies were erected when the overall roof was removed. Despite being Listed structures, the office and waiting room on the up side were destroyed in 1978. (T.Heavyside)

108. We now have two photographs from 2nd June 1980. Platform 3 (right) was subsequently renumbered 1a and 1b and is signalled for reversible running. In the background are five carriage sidings and the former MR goods shed. (T.Heavyside)

109.   The luggage lifts serving the nearest bridge are featured in this photograph of no. 47467 arriving from Paddington on the same day. Locomotive haulage has been rare since the introduction of Thames Turbos in the mid-1990s. (T.Heavyside)

110.   No. 33116 was an unusual sight on 14th August 1993. It was working the 08.39 Waterloo to Kidderminster "Push Pull Tours". The signal lamps were still oil lit. These, together with others locally, required the service of a full time lampman. (P.G.Barnes)

111.   We finish our survey of the station with three views from March 2003. The north end is seen from a departing train, with the former goods shed in the background. Also evident are the two goods lines that bypass the station. There had been a signal box in the left background until August 1968. It had 30 levers and was named "Goods Yard". (V.Mitchell)

112.   A notable architectural gem to survive the general clearance of historic railway artefacts is the former buffet on the up platform. Its exquisite tiling in subtle colours is worthy of a special journey. (V.Mitchell)

113.   The desolate scene southwards does at least include an operational signal box. Many sidings were still in place, including one to the massive Metal Box works, hidden by the mist in the distance. Its private siding was still in use in 2003. (V.Mitchell)

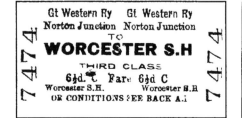

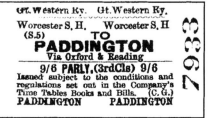

114.   Reference to map XXVI will confirm that this is a southward view from its top left area. On the right, we look between the two engine sheds, the clear track to the right of the coal wagons leading to Shrub Hill, the one to the right of it serving the Vinegar Works and other industries. On the left of this 1894 panorama is the former OWWR locomotive works, which the GWR used for major repairs. (LGRP/NRM)

115.   The three-road shed was photographed from the south on 19th June 1960. Centre is no. 6812 *Chesford Grange* and on the right is 0-6-0PT no. 4614. The loco works closed on 1st October 1964 and the sheds followed in December 1965. (P.J.Kelley)

116.   The three-road shed was retained as part of the diesel depot, but when photographed from the down platform in August 1985, one doorway had been bricked up and the roof had been removed. The sidings were still in use for DMU stabling in 2003, but there was little evidence of the old buildings. (P.G.Barnes)

3. Long Marston Branch

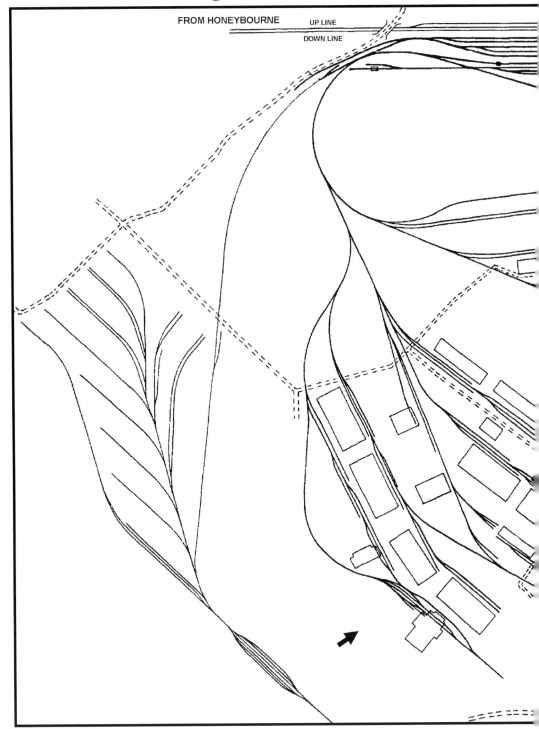

FROM HONEYBOURNE   UP LINE

DOWN LINE

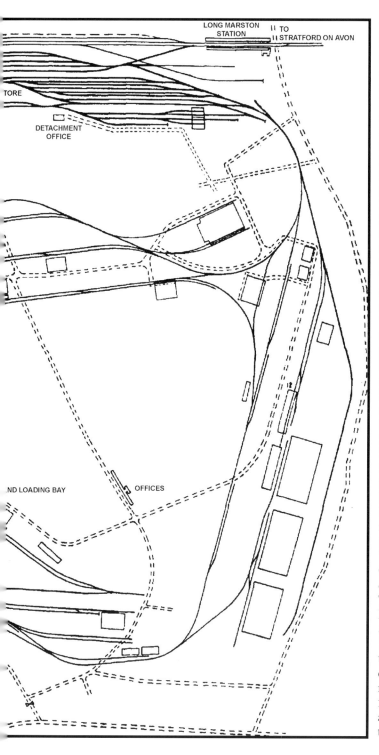

LONG MARSTON
STATION

II TO
II STRATFORD ON AVON

TORE

DETACHMENT
OFFICE

ND LOADING BAY

OFFICES

XXVIII. A 1967 plan includes the station (top right). This closed to goods on 7th September 1964 and to passengers on 3rd January 1966. The route northwards to Stratford-upon-Avon closed completely on 1st November 1976. The up refuge siding is shown as a dotted line and the thicker lines represent those belonging to the Ministry of Defence. The massive stores depot was laid out in 1940 on a 455 acre site. The track mileage was eventually in excess of 25 and there were 136 points. The area of the left page with thinner lines was purchased by Birds Commercial Motors for use as a breakers yard. Many items of railway stock met their end here, but the site has been redeveloped since 2001. The remainder of the former depot was prepared for sale that year, it then being known as Central Engineer Park. The four-road engine shed, near the station, was used by the Yorkshire Engine Company in the 1990s for diesel locomotive repairs. The Stratford on Avon, Broadway Railway Society was formed in 1995 to secure the future of the route. The group collected some items of rolling stock and arranged for the use of the two sheds and some of the sidings at the top of the plan.

117. Two views from 5th October 1994 show retired NSE stock in store prior to disposal. This panorama is from the road bridge and includes the PW Store, which was later used by the SBR for carriage repairs. (M.J.Stretton)

118.   Looking east from the bridge approach, we see no. 309605, an EMU that spent most of its life in Essex. The shed on the left was used for carriage and wagon repairs and later became the SBR's engine shed. (M.J.Stretton)

119.   Andrew Barclay diesel no. 42 was one of 15 similar 0-4-0s to be landed in Normandy, soon after D-Day (see *Railways to Victory*). It is named *Overlord*, after this remarkable military operation. Also present were the SBR's sister locomotive, no. 201 *Mulberry* and Fowler no. 4 *Chorley*. (M.Hall)

120.   The scene from the road bridge on 14th August 2003 was one of increasing desolation The main line had been on the left and the track running to the gate was laid in 1981 to connect the former down line with the exchange sidings. There was little railway activity by the time that this photograph was taken, but the route from Honeybourne was still intact. (M.J.Stretton)

Other views of this area, including the station, can be seen in pictures 27 to 37 in *Stratford-upon-Avon to Cheltenham*.

MP Middleton Press

Easebourne Lane, Midhurst, W Sussex. GU29 9AZ Tel: 01730 813169 Fax: 01730 812601
Email: sales@middletonpress.co.uk   www.middletonpress.co.uk
If books are not available from your local transport stockist, order direct post free UK.

BRANCH LINES
Branch Line to Allhallows
Branch Line to Alton
Branch Lines around Ascot
Branch Line to Ashburton
Branch Lines around Bodmin
Branch Line to Bude
Branch Lines around Canterbury
Branch Lines around Chard & Yeovil
Branch Line to Cheddar
Branch Lines around Cromer
Branch Line to the Derwent Valley
Branch Lines to East Grinstead
Branch Lines of East London
Branch Lines to Effingham Junction
Branch Lines around Exmouth
Branch Lines to Falmouth, Helston & St. Ives
Branch Line to Fairford
Branch Lines to Felixstow & Aldeburgh
Branch Lines around Gosport
Branch Line to Hayling
Branch Lines to Henley, Windsor & Marlow
Branch Line to Hawkhurst
Branch Line to Horsham
Branch Lines around Huntingdon
Branch Line to Kingsbridge
Branch Line to Kingswear
Branch Line to Lambourn
Branch Lines to Launceston & Princetown
Branch Lines to Longmoor
Branch Line to Looe
Branch Line to Lyme Regis
Branch Line to Lynton
Branch Lines around March
Branch Lines around Midhurst
Branch Line to Minehead
Branch Line to Moretonhampstead
Branch Lines to Newport (IOW)
Branch Lines to Newquay
Branch Lines around North Woolwich
Branch Line to Padstow
Branch Lines to Princes Risborough
Branch Lines to Seaton and Sidmouth
Branch Lines around Sheerness
Branch Line to Shrewsbury
Branch Line to Tenterden
Branch Lines around Tiverton
Branch Lines to Torrington
Branch Lines to Tunbridge Wells
Branch Line to Upwell
Branch Lines of West London
Branch Lines of West Wiltshire
Branch Lines around Weymouth
Branch Lines around Wimborne
Branch Lines around Wisbech

NARROW GAUGE
Austrian Narrow Gauge
Branch Line to Lynton
Branch Lines around Portmadoc 1923-46
Branch Lines around Porthmadog 1954-94
Branch Line to Southwold
Douglas to Port Erin
Douglas to Peel
Kent Narrow Gauge
Northern France Narrow Gauge
Romneyrail
Southern France Narrow Gauge
Sussex Narrow Gauge
Surrey Narrow Gauge
Swiss Narrow Gauge
Two-Foot Gauge Survivors
Vivarais Narrow Gauge

SOUTH COAST RAILWAYS
Ashford to Dover
Bournemouth to Weymouth
Brighton to Worthing
Dover to Ramsgate
Eastbourne to Hastings
Hastings to Ashford
Portsmouth to Southampton
Ryde to Ventnor
Southampton to Bournemouth

SOUTHERN MAIN LINES
Basingstoke to Salisbury
Crawley to Littlehampton
Dartford to Sittingbourne
East Croydon to Three Bridges
Epsom to Horsham
Exeter to Barnstaple
Exeter to Tavistock
London Bridge to East Croydon
Orpington to Tonbridge
Tonbridge to Hastings
Salisbury to Yeovil
Sittingbourne to Ramsgate
Swanley to Ashford
Tavistock to Plymouth
Three Bridges to Brighton
Victoria to Bromley South
Victoria to East Croydon
Waterloo to Windsor
Waterloo to Woking
Woking to Portsmouth
Woking to Southampton
Yeovil to Exeter

EASTERN MAIN LINES
Barking to Southend
Ely to Kings Lynn
Ely to Norwich
Fenchurch Street to Barking
Hitchin to Peterborough
Ilford to Shenfield
Ipswich to Saxmundham
Liverpool Street to Ilford
Saxmundham to Yarmouth
Tilbury Loop

WESTERN MAIN LINES
Bristol to Taunton
Didcot to Banbury
Didcot to Swindon
Ealing to Slough
Exeter to Newton Abbot
Newton Abbot to Plymouth
Newbury to Westbury
Oxford to Moreton-in-Marsh
Paddington to Ealing
Paddington to Princes Risborough
Plymouth to St. Austell
Princes Risborough to Banbury
Reading to Didcot
Slough to Newbury
St. Austell to Penzance
Swindon to Bristol
Taunton to Exeter
Westbury to Taunton

MIDLAND MAIN LINES
St. Albans to Bedford
Euston to Harrow & Wealdstone
Harrow to Watford
St. Pancras to St. Albans

COUNTRY RAILWAY ROUTES
Abergavenny to Merthyr
Andover to Southampton
Bath to Evercreech Junction
Bath Green Park to Bristol
Bournemouth to Evercreech Junction
Brecon to Newport
Burnham to Evercreech Junction
Cheltenham to Andover
Croydon to East Grinstead
Didcot to Winchester
East Kent Light Railway
Frome to Bristol
Guildford to Redhill
Reading to Basingstoke
Reading to Guildford
Redhill to Ashford
Salisbury to Westbury
Stratford upon Avon to Cheltenham
Strood to Paddock Wood
Taunton to Barnstaple
Wenford Bridge to Fowey
Westbury to Bath
Woking to Alton
Yeovil to Dorchester

GREAT RAILWAY ERAS
Ashford from Steam to Eurostar
Clapham Junction 50 years of change
Festiniog in the Fifties
Festiniog in the Sixties
Festiniog 50 years of enterprise
Isle of Wight Lines 50 years of change
Railways to Victory 1944-46
Return to Blaenau 1970-82
SECR Centenary album
Talyllyn 50 years of change
Wareham to Swanage 50 years of change
Yeovil 50 years of change

LONDON SUBURBAN RAILWAYS
Caterham and Tattenham Corner
Charing Cross to Dartford
Clapham Jn. to Beckenham Jn.
Crystal Palace (HL) & Catford Loop
East London Line
Finsbury Park to Alexandra Palace
Holborn Viaduct to Lewisham
Kingston and Hounslow Loops
Lewisham to Dartford
Liverpool Street to Chingford
London Bridge to Addiscombe
Mitcham Junction Lines
North London Line
South London Line
West Croydon to Epsom
West London Line
Willesden Junction to Richmond
Wimbledon to Beckenham
Wimbledon to Epsom

STEAMING THROUGH
Steaming through Cornwall
Steaming through the Isle of Wight
Steaming through Kent
Steaming through West Hants

TRAMWAY CLASSICS
Aldgate & Stepney Tramways
Barnet & Finchley Tramways
Bath Tramways
Brighton's Tramways
Bristol's Tramways
Burton & Ashby Tramways
Camberwell & W.Norwood Tramways
Clapham & Streatham Tramways
Croydon's Tramways
Dover's Tramways
East Ham & West Ham Tramways
Edgware and Willesden Tramways
Eltham & Woolwich Tramways
Embankment & Waterloo Tramways
Exeter & Taunton Tramways
Fulwell - Home to Trams, Trolleys and Buses
Great Yarmouth Tramways
Greenwich & Dartford Tramways
Hammersmith & Hounslow Tramways
Hampstead & Highgate Tramways
Hastings Tramways
Holborn & Finsbury Tramways
Ilford & Barking Tramways
Kingston & Wimbledon Tramways
Lewisham & Catford Tramways
Liverpool Tramways 1. Eastern Routes
Liverpool Tramways 2. Southern Routes
Liverpool Tramways 3. Northern Routes
Maidstone & Chatham Tramways
Margate to Ramsgate
North Kent Tramways
Norwich Tramways
Reading Tramways
Seaton & Eastbourne Tramways
Shepherds Bush & Uxbridge Tramways
Southend-on-sea Tramways
South London Line Tramways 1903-33
Southwark & Deptford Tramways
Stamford Hill Tramways
Twickenham & Kingston Tramways
Victoria & Lambeth Tramways
Waltham Cross & Edmonton Tramways
Walthamstow & Leyton Tramways
Wandsworth & Battersea Tramways

TROLLEYBUS CLASSICS
Bradford Trolleybuses
Croydon Trolleybuses
Derby Trolleybuses
Hastings Trolleybuses
Huddersfield Trolleybuses
Maidstone Trolleybuses
Portsmouth Trolleybuses
Reading Trolleybuses

WATERWAY ALBUMS
Kent and East Sussex Waterways
London to Portsmouth Waterway
West Sussex Waterways

MILITARY BOOKS
Battle over Portsmouth
Battle over Sussex 1940
Blitz over Sussex 1941-42
Bombers over Sussex 1943-45
Bognor at War
Military Defence of West Sussex
Military Signals from the South Coast
Secret Sussex Resistance
Surrey Home Guard

OTHER RAILWAY BOOKS
Index to all Middleton Press stations
Industrial Railways of the South-East
South Eastern & Chatham Railways
London Chatham & Dover Railway
London Termini - Past and Proposed
War on the Line (SR 1939-45)